Energy Essentials

Fossil Fuel

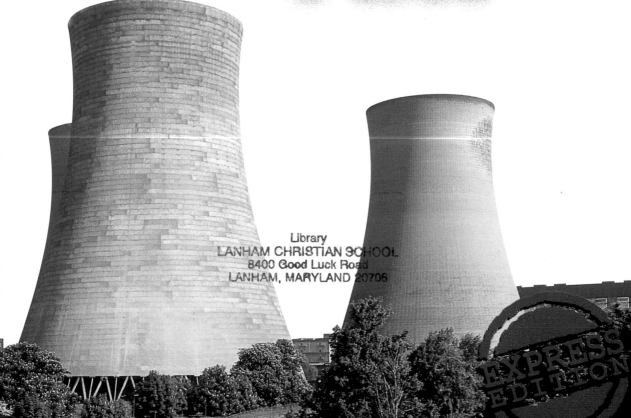

EXPRESS EDITION

Nigel Saunders and Steven Chapman

Raintree

For information, address the publisher:
Raintree, 100 N. LaSalle, Suite 1200, Chicago, IL 60602

Printed and bound in China
10 09 08 07 06
10 9 8 7 6 5 4 3 2

Library of Congress Cataloging-in-Publication Data

Saunders, N. (Nigel)
  Fossil fuel / Nigel Saunders and Steven Chapman.
    p. cm. -- (Energy essentials)
  Includes bibliographical references and index.
  ISBN 1-4109-1693-6 (lib. bdg.) -- ISBN 1-4109-1698-7 (pbk.)
  ISBN 978-1-4109-1693-8 (HC) -- ISBN 978-1-4109-1698-3 (pbk)
  1. Fossil fuels--Juvenile literature. I. Chapman, Steven. II. Title.
  TP318.3.S43 2005
  333.8'2--dc22
                          2005003648

This leveled text is a version of Freestyle: Energy Essentials: Fossil
Fuels.

Acknowledgments

p.4/5, Science Photo Library; p.4, Science Photo Library/
D. Ouelette, Publiphoto Diffusion; p.5 (top)Corbis; p.5 (mid)
Science Photo Library; p.5 (bottom), Science Photo library
Zedcor/James Holmes; p.6/7, Science Photo Library; p.6, Corbis;
p.7, Science Photo Library/Chris Butler; pp.8/9, Alamy; p.8,
Science Photo Library; p.9, Oxford Scientfic Films; pp.10/11,
Science Photo Library; p.10, Corbis; p.11, Oxford Scientfic Films;
p.12/13, Corbis; p.12, Corbis; p.13, Corbis; p.14 (top), Heritage
Images/ Science Museum/HIP/ Topfoto; p.14 (bottom), Science
Photo Library; p.15, Corbis; p.16 left, Photodisc; p.16 right,
Science Photo Library; p.17, Corbis/ Paul A Sonders; p.18 (top),
Science Photo Library; p.18 (bottom), Oxford Scientfic Films; p.19,
Corbis; p.20 (top), Corbis; p.20 (bottom), Science Photo Library;
p.21, Rex Features; pp.22/23, photodisc; p.22, Science Photo
Library/Vanessa Vick; p.24, Science Photo Library/ Martin Bond;
p.25, Science Photo library Zedcor/James Holmes; p.26, Science
Photo Library; p.27, Science Photo Library/Ben Johnson;
pp.28/29, Science Photo Library; p.29, Science Photo Library; p.30
(right), Science Photo Library; p.30 (left), Science Photo Library;
p.31, Corbis; p.32, Science Photo Library; p.34 (top), Corbis/
Document General Motors/Reuter R; p.34 (bottom), Science Photo
Library; p.35, Science Photo Library/ Simon Fraser; pp.36/37,
Getty Images News and Sport; pp.38/39, Science Photo Library;
p.38, Getty Images News and Sport; p.39, Oxford Scientfic Films;
pp.40–41, Ecoscene; p.40, Science Photo Library; p.41, Science
Photo Library/ Martin Bond; p.42 (right), Science Photo Library;
p.42 (left), Getty Images News and Sport; p.43, Rex
Features/Stewart Cook.

Cover photograph of gas hob reproduced with permission of Getty
Imagebank

Contents

Any words appearing in the text in bold, **like this**, are explained in the Glossary. You can also look for them in the Word Store at the bottom of each page.

What are Fuels?

A fuel is anything that gives off heat or another kind of **energy** when it burns. Fuels store energy. We can turn energy into heat or light or sound. Fuels can also be used to make things move. One important use of fuels is to make electricity.

Bad fuels

Not all things that burn are good fuels. The rubber car tires shown below burn easily. They are not good fuels because they produce thick, black smoke and poisonous gases.

Word Store   energy   being able to do work. Light, heat, and electricity are types of energy

Fossil fuels

Have you ever seen a fossil? A fossil is the remains of a plant or animal that lived millions of years ago. **Fossil fuels** are the **fossilized** remains of plants and animals that store energy in a form that we can use. There are three types of fossil fuel: coal, oil, and natural gas. This book will tell you all about them.

Find out later ...

. . . how these machines dig.

. . . what huge oil platforms do.

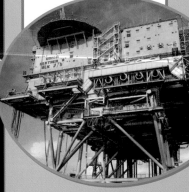

. . . what fossil fuels are used for.

▲ Tankers like this are used to carry fuels such as oil or natural gas around the world.

fossil fuel   fuel formed from the remains of ancient plants and animals

Coal

Swamps

This is a swamp. It is similar to those in which coal formed millions of years ago.

Coal is a type of **fossilized** rock. It is made from the remains of ancient plants that lived millions of years ago.

Sunlight makes forests

About 300 million years ago, the world was a very different place. It was much warmer than it is today. The land was covered by huge, swampy forests.

The trees and other plants in the forests captured the **energy** from the Sun and stored it.

Word Store fossilized turned into stone

The forests die

When the plants that grew in these swampy forests died, they did not rot away. Instead, thick layers of plants formed as dead plants fell on top of each other. These layers of plants were then slowly buried by layers of mud and sand.

Plants to coal

Over millions of years, the plant layers slowly turned into coal. The Sun's energy that was stored in the trees remains in the layers of coal.

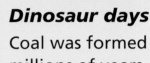

Dinosaur days
Coal was formed millions of years before dinosaurs lived on Earth.

◄ Earth was warmer 300 million years ago. Plants grew very quickly in swamps like these.

Peat

Peat is a type of fuel made from the remains of **bog** plants that have been buried for thousands of years. It is dug up out of the ground and dried before being burned.

Types of coal

Several different types of coal were formed. The type depended on how long the coal was buried and how deep. Coal is mostly made of **carbon**. The more carbon there is in coal, the better it burns and the less **pollution** it makes.

Anthracite

Anthracite is nearly pure carbon and is the best type of coal. It is hard, black, and shiny. When it burns, it gives off lots of heat.

carbon   type of chemical

Bituminous coal

The most common type of coal is called bituminous coal. It can be soft and powdery or hard and shiny. It burns with a hot flame but makes a lot of smoke.

Lignite

Lignite has the least amount of carbon of all coals. It gives off the least heat and makes the most smoke. It is mainly used in **power stations** to make electricity.

Fossilized leaves

It is sometimes possible to find **fossilized** leaves in pieces of coal.

▼ This is anthracite burning.

Mining coal

A layer of coal is called a coal **seam**. Where the coal seams are near the surface, the coal can be removed by surface mining. Huge digging machines remove the soil and rock that lie on top of the coal. The coal can then be dug up.

▼ This surface mine is in Germany. The coal from it is used in a nearby **power station**.

Mining machines

Huge machines are needed to remove the soil and rock in surface mining. A digger, such as the one below, can scoop up more than 100 cubic yards (90 cubic meters) of soil, at one time.

Land reclamation

Surface mining can do a lot of damage to the **environment**. To reduce this damage, the land can be **reclaimed** after the mining work is finished. This means the rock and soil that were taken away are put back. Then trees, bushes, and grasses are planted. Some reclaimed land is made into parks for both wildlife and people.

Reclaiming the land

The picture above shows an area of land that has been reclaimed after surface mining.

reclaim   make something useful again

Underground mining

If a **seam** of coal is very deep, it is mined from deep under the ground.

Underground mining can be dangerous for the miners. Deep holes called **shafts** are dug, and the miners have to work deep underground. Coal is cut from the **coalface** by special cutting tools. Then **conveyor belts** carry it back to the shafts where it is lifted to the surface.

Pit ponies

Many years ago, pit ponies and children were used to pull the coal out of mines.

coalface   part of a coal seam that is being cut away

Room and pillar mining

If all the coal was removed from a seam, the mine would collapse. To stop this from happening, the miners leave some thick coal pillars to hold up the roof. These are surrounded by "rooms" where the coal has been removed. This means it is less dangerous for the miners. But only about half the coal in a seam can actually be mined.

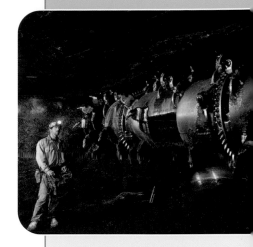

▼ About two-thirds of the world's coal is mined by underground mining.

Longwall mining

In longwall mining (above), spinning blades cut the coal and the roof is held up by machines. After the coal has been taken away, the roof is allowed to cave in. Unfortunately, this often causes the land above to **subside**.

subside   sink downward

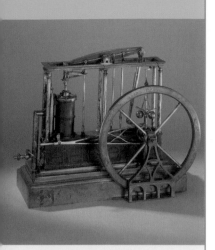

The steam engine

This is a model of one of the first steam engines. It was built by James Watt in 1769.

Steam power

Just over 200 years ago, there were very few machines in the world. Most machines were powered by horses or people. However, the invention of the steam engine allowed powered machinery and transportation.

The fuel that steam engines and machines used was coal. This was the age of the **Industrial Revolution**. It began in Britain, and quickly spread to other parts of the world.

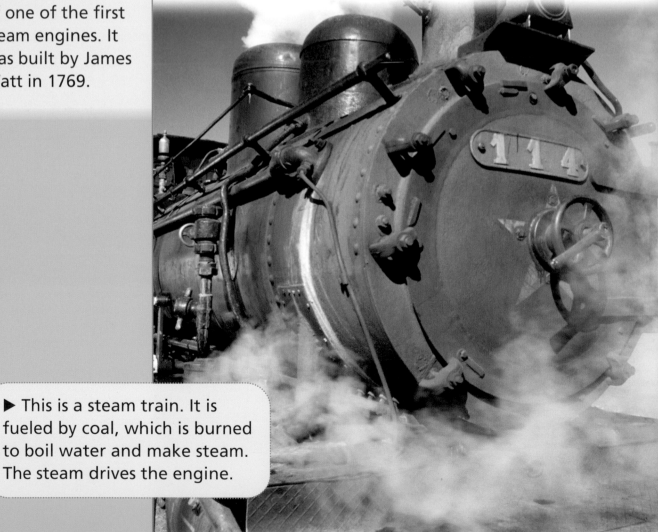

▶ This is a steam train. It is fueled by coal, which is burned to boil water and make steam. The steam drives the engine.

Industrial Revolution period of rapid development in industry in the late 1700s and early 1800s

Problems with coal

During the Industrial Revolution, coal powered almost everything. However, burning coal created smoke—this is a mixture of gas and unburned **particles** of fuel.

Smoke makes it difficult for people to breathe. It can also turn trees and buildings black. Burning coal has caused a lot of damage to the **environment**.

Killer smog

In London, England, in December 1952 smoke from homes and factories mixed with fog to make a thick, black **smog**. It was almost impossible to see. Buses had to be guided by people holding white flags (left). About 4,000 people died of breathing problems.

smog   mixture of smoke and fog

▲ These are the cooling towers of a power station. The "smoke" escaping from them is in fact harmless steam.

Stop pollution

Old coal-fired power stations like the one below were very **polluting**. Now, power stations have **filters** attached to their chimneys to stop the ash and gases in the smoke from escaping.

Coal today

Today, people around the world use more and more coal. Some is used to make machines work or heat homes. The biggest use of coal today is in **power stations**, where coal is used to make electricity.

Making electricity

In a power station, coal is burned to give off heat **energy**. This heat boils water to make steam. The steam powers a **generator** that makes electricity.

Other uses of coal

If coal is heated to a high temperature it produces coke, coal gas, and coal tar. Coke makes a good fuel that is used in making **steel**.

Coal gas can be burned like natural gas for heating and lighting. Coal tar is a mixture of many substances. Some of these are used to make dyes, paints, varnishes, soaps, medicines, and **pesticides**. Coal tar is also used to make road surfaces.

Steelmaking
Coke is an important **raw material** in the steelmaking process. This man is pouring **molten steel** at a steel plant in Canada.

steel   metal made from iron

Oil

Like coal, oil is formed from the remains of ancient living things. But while coal is formed from plants, oil is formed from the remains of tiny sea creatures.

Millions of years ago when these creatures died, they sank to the bottom of the sea. Layers of mud and sand then covered them. Over millions of years, they turned into oil.

▼ Getting oil out of the ground is very messy work.

Oil and water

Oil and water do not mix. Oil does not mix with water but floats on top of it. This is why you often see swirling patterns of oil on puddles of water beside the road (above).

oilfield   reservoir of oil underground

Oilfields and tar pits

The oil formed into huge underground **oilfields**. In some areas where the rock is **porous,** the oil is able to work its way up through the rocks to the surface. When the oil reaches the surface, sticky areas called tar pits are formed.

Animal traps

In the past, animals have fallen into tar pits and drowned. The tar pits at Rancho La Brea in California (left) contain the bones of saber-toothed tigers and other ancient animals that lived more than 30,000 years ago.

porous   lets liquids and gases through

Looking for oil

Geologists are scientists who study rocks. To find oil, they look at information about the rocks underground. They look for layers of rock where oil could be trapped.

Once the geologists have found a good place to look for oil, a drilling **rig** makes test holes.

Searching for oil

Sometimes satellites in space are used to search for oil.

▼ Giant oil rigs and platforms are used to drill for oil at sea.

rig   large structure used to extract oil from under the ground or the seabed

Finding oil at sea

If the drilling test finds oil under the sea, a huge oil platform is built. A well more than one-third of a mile (several hundred meters) deep is then dug. The well is lined with steel to stop it from collapsing.

The top of the well is sealed with strong **valves** to stop the oil from escaping. The valves allow the flow of oil to be turned on and off. The oil flows in pipes to storage tanks onshore.

Blowout!

Sometimes the oil forces its way out of the well and sprays over the drilling rig like a fountain. This is called a blowout. In this blowout at sea, the oil is being burned on the surface of the sea.

valve   switch for controlling the movement of liquid, or gas, through a pipe

Oil refining

Oil cannot be used straight from the well. It is **refined** at an oil refinery, where it is separated into its different parts.

At the refinery

At the oil refinery, the oil is heated to a very high temperature. It is then pumped into the bottom of a tall, metal tower. This is very hot at the bottom and gets cooler higher up.

Oil spills

Sometimes the big tankers that carry oil run aground and spill their oil. When this happens, the thick, black oil **pollutes** the sea, kills wildlife, and ruins beaches.

▼ Different fuels are separated out from crude oil at oil refineries and stored in large containers.

Fractions

The substances in the oil **evaporate**, and their **vapors** rise up the tower. Substances with high boiling points, such as diesel, are the first to **condense** near the bottom of the tower. Substances with low boiling points rise higher up the tower (see the diagram on page 25).

As each vapor condenses and turns back to a liquid, it is collected. The different substances that are separated out in this way are called **fractions**.

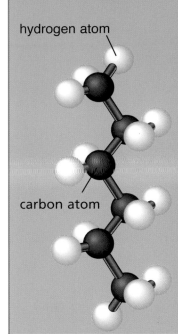

hydrogen atom

carbon atom

Hydrocarbons

The substances in oil are called hydrocarbons. This means that their **molecules** are made from hydrogen and **carbon atoms**. This is a model of a hydrocarbon found in oil.

Oil for almost everything

The **fractions** of oil have an amazing range of uses. Many are used as fuels. Others are used as **raw materials** in the chemical industry.

The residue

The material at the bottom of the tower is called the residue. It contains tar, which is used to make road surfaces. Tar is also used to make paraffin waxes, candles, and polishes.

A thick liquid called fuel oil is also found in the residue. This is a good fuel for ships and **power stations**.

Fuels for land and air

Gasoline, diesel, and kerosene are all found in oil. They are used as fuel—gasoline for cars, kerosene for airplanes, and diesel for cars, trains, trolleys, and buses.

Four useful gases

Butane, propane, methane, and ethane come off the top of the tower.

Cracking oil

This is a cracking plant. It changes substances in oil into new liquids such as gasoline. This process is called "cracking."

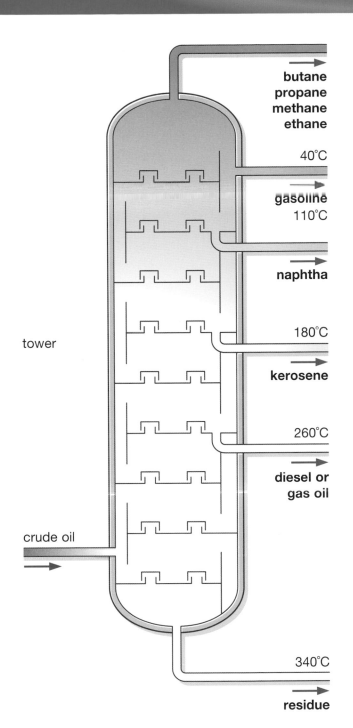

butane
propane
methane
ethane

40°C

tower

gasoline
110°C

naphtha

180°C

kerosene

260°C

diesel or
gas oil

crude oil

340°C

residue

▲ These are the main substances
separated from oil in an oil refinery.

Making things with naphtha

The gas naphtha is also taken out of oil. Naphtha is used for making many things like soaps, rubber, and medicines. Plastics such as polythene (above) are also made using naphtha.

Natural Gas

Natural gas is formed in the same way as oil. Oil and gas are often found together. A layer of **nonporous** rock always lies above them, trapping them underground.

Gas and oil are removed from the ground in the same way. A well is dug deep into the ground. If a well collects enough oil or gas to be useful, it is called a productive well. A well that collects little or no gas is considered a dry well.

Methane

When dead plants and animals rot, they give off methane gas. This can cause explosions in **landfill** garbage dumps. To stop this from happening, vents (holes) have to be left to allow the gas to escape. Here, a scientist measures the amount of gas given off at a landfill vent.

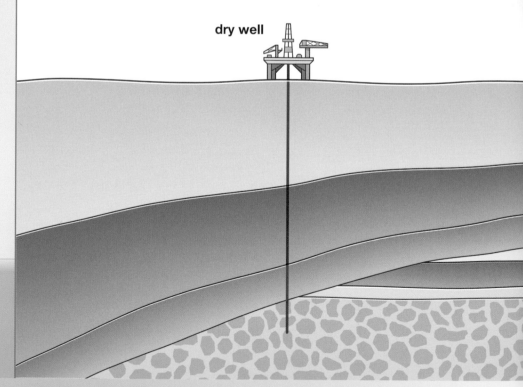

dry well

nonporous   does not let liquid and gases through

Separating natural gas

Natural gas is usually sent from the gas fields to a refinery through pipelines. At the refinery, the natural gas is separated into propane, butane, methane, and ethane.

Natural gas is mostly methane, and it is what we use in our houses. Methane has no smell, color, or taste. It is also very dangerous. Gas companies add a smelly chemical to it so that people can smell if they have a gas leak.

▼ One of these wells has found an area of oil and gas. This is a productive well. The other well is a dry well and has not found fuel.

productive well

nonporous rock

gas

oil

porous rock

water pushes the gas and oil upward

Safety underground

Natural gas can leak into coal mines. Early miners needed to bring in lamps. The flame in the lamp could cause an explosion and kill the miners. Sir Humphry Davy invented a safety lamp for miners (below). This lamp could be brought into a mine without the risk of causing an explosion.

landfill   waste site

Pipelines

Natural gas is carried all over the world in a huge network of underground pipelines. Powerful pumps push the gas through large pipes. The pipes branch off in towns and cities. They become narrower at each branch until the gas enters a house, office, or factory in a narrow plastic pipe.

The gas starts its journey at a very high **pressure**. This would be dangerous because it would be hard to stop leaks in the home. By the time it reaches your house, the pressure is reduced to a safer level.

Bunsen burner

The Bunsen burner was invented by German scientists Gustav Kirchhoff and Robert Bunsen in the middle of the 1800s. The Bunsen burner burns natural gas and is used for science experiments (above).

▼ One of the main uses of natural gas in our homes is for cooking.

pressure   amount of force pushing on something

Uses of natural gas

Natural gas is used in homes, schools, offices, restaurants, and hotels for:

- cooking;
- heating water;
- running air conditioning systems.

It is used in factories for:

- heating;
- air conditioning;
- as a **raw material** in chemical making.

It is also used in gas-fired **power stations** as a fuel to make electricity.

Driving with gas

Natural gas can be used as a fuel for vehicles. Here, a bus refuels at a special gas station.

---

power station   place where electricity is generated

Problems with Fossil Fuels

Fossil fuels may be very important to us, but they have two big problems. When we use them, they cause **pollution** to our **environment**, and they are running out.

Sulfur dioxide

When fossil fuels burn, they release a gas called sulfur dioxide into the air. Sulfur dioxide **dissolves** in rain water to make **acid rain**.

Volcanoes

Sulfur dioxide is also released into the air by volcanoes. Mount St. Helens in Washington (above) gave off almost 450,000 short tons (400,000 metric tonnes) of sulfur dioxide when it erupted in 1980.

▼ Acid rain has damaged this sculpture of a lion.

acid rain   rain that contains substances that damage buildings and living things

Acid rain

Acid rain damages the environment in many ways. It dissolves metals and the stone surfaces of buildings and statues. When acid rain falls on the soil, it removes important **minerals** from the soil. Trees and plants can no longer grow well, and eventually die. When the acid rain reaches rivers and lakes, it can kill both plants and animals.

▼ This boat is spraying powdered lime onto a lake polluted by acid rain. The lime **neutralizes** the effect of the acid rain.

Beating acid rain

To stop acid rain, the smoke from power stations can be filtered to remove the sulfur dioxide. Also the sulfur can be taken away from the fuels before they are burned.

neutralize   make a substance neutral, not acid or alkali

Cows and rice fields

Methane is the main gas in natural gas. It is also a greenhouse gas. Methane is given off in large quantities by grazing animals and also by growing rice (above).

The greenhouse effect

Earth is kept warm by its **atmosphere**. This is the layer of gases that surrounds Earth. If there were no atmosphere, Earth would be a cold place.

The gases in the atmosphere trap heat **energy** from the Sun. These gases work in the same way as the glass on a greenhouse, so we call them greenhouse gases. Carbon dioxide, which is found naturally in the atmosphere, is the most important greenhouse gas. Keeping Earth warm in this way is called the **greenhouse effect**.

▼ The greenhouse effect means that some of the Sun's heat energy is trapped by the gases in the atmosphere.

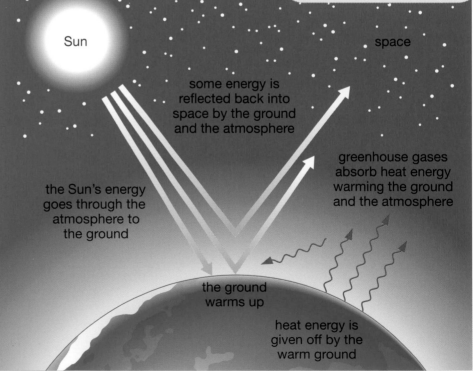

Sun

space

some energy is reflected back into space by the ground and the atmosphere

greenhouse gases absorb heat energy warming the ground and the atmosphere

the Sun's energy goes through the atmosphere to the ground

the ground warms up

heat energy is given off by the warm ground

atmosphere   the layer of gases that surrounds the planet

Global warming

The burning of **fossil fuels** means that a lot of extra carbon dioxide is released into the atmosphere. Many scientists believe that the extra carbon dioxide traps more heat and makes the greenhouse effect stronger than normal. Because of this, temperatures are rising all over the world. This is called **global warming**.

Carbon dioxide levels

The graph below shows how the level of carbon dioxide has risen in the last 140 years. The average temperature on Earth has also gone up during this time.

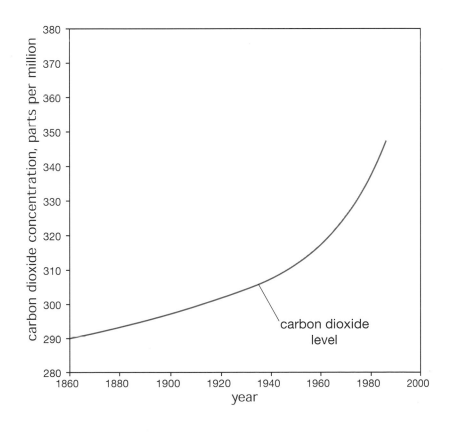

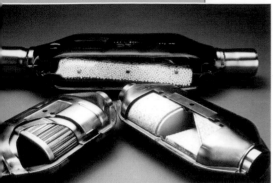

Catalytic converters

Catalytic converters (above) are fitted to car exhaust pipes to remove some of the polluting gases.

Exhaust fumes

All gasoline and diesel engines create a large amount of **polluting** gases. These are released into the **atmosphere** through the vehicle's exhaust pipe.

The largest part of exhaust fumes is carbon monoxide. This is a very poisonous gas. Other gases, such as nitrogen, help make **acid rain**.

▼ The waste gases from car exhaust pipes are unpleasant, and they pollute the air we breathe.

Ozone

Ozone is a gas. When it is high up in the atmosphere, it shields us from harmful **ultraviolet light** from the Sun. However, at ground level it causes stinging eyes and breathing problems. Sunlight makes the different substances in exhaust fumes **react** with each other to make ozone. This causes a big problem in cities on summer days. Ozone can also be moved by the wind to the countryside, where it damages growing crops.

Modern smog

Smog is a nasty mixture of harmful materials in the air. Smog can travel long distances away from the cities where it forms. In the picture below, the smog has traveled hundreds of miles (hundreds of kilometers) from the city of Los Angeles, California to the mountains.

ultraviolet light   invisible light that can damage skin, eyes, and growing plants

Type of fossil fuel	Coal	Oil	Natural gas
Time left until it runs out	214 years	39 years	61 years

Some guesses

The chart above shows when coal, oil, and natural gas are expected to run out. Scientists think that we have already used half the world's supply of oil, so we will probably run out of this first.

Running out

Could we live without **fossil fuels**? The answer is simple—yes. They are running out and one day we will have to. Fossil fuels are **nonrenewable energy** resources. This means they cannot be replaced.

We need to find other sources of fuels—preferably **renewable** ones.

▼ As fossil fuels run out, empty gas stations may become a familiar sight.

New locations

Although new coal, oil, and gas fields are discovered each year, the number of new sites is decreasing. As fossil fuels begin to run out, their price will rise. Sites that are considered too difficult and expensive to reach at the moment will soon become worth exploring.

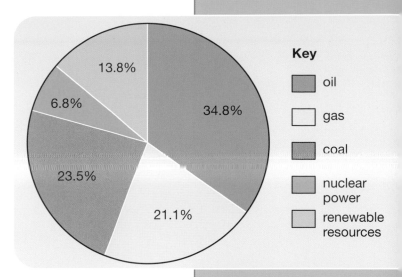

Key

- oil
- gas
- coal
- nuclear power
- renewable resources

Other resources

Right now, about 80 percent of the world's energy comes from fossil fuels. The pie chart above shows the types of energy used in the world at the moment.

renewable   will not run out and can be replaced

What Next?

It is important to remember that **fossil fuels** are not just used as **energy resources**. They are also important **raw materials**. Once the fossil fuels have gone, many useful substances will have to be made from something else.

Plant power

Plants are already a very useful source of raw materials. From them we get wood, rubber, cork, and many medicines. Soon, we might be running our cars on plant oil. The seeds of some plants contain vegetable oil, which can be changed into a fuel called "biodiesel."

Hydrogen fuel

Hydrogen is a gas that burns very easily and can be used to fuel cars, such as the one above. However, hydrogen is very explosive and is difficult to store and handle.

▲ Nuclear power stations make electricity without using fossil fuels.

energy resource   something from which we can get useful amounts of energy

Nuclear energy

Nuclear energy is the energy stored inside **atoms**. Inside a nuclear **power station**, atoms of uranium are split. This releases enormous amounts of heat energy, which is then used to make steam, turn turbines, and generate electricity.

Uranium

Uranium is the metal that is the raw material in nuclear power stations. Although it creates a very useful form of energy, it also gives out invisible energy that is very dangerous to living things.

Geothermal energy

It is very hot inside Earth. **Geothermal** power stations, such as the one below, use this heat to provide energy. Hot water from underground is pumped to the surface, where it can be used to heat houses or generate electricity.

Renewable energy resources

Renewable energy resources include **solar power**, wind power, and **hydroelectric power**.

Wind power

Wind power has been used for centuries to provide **energy**. Today, wind farms consist of rows and rows of wind **turbines**. Wind turbines do not create **pollution**, although some people who live near them do not like the noise they make.

Solar power

Solar power stations use the energy from the Sun to **generate** electricity. In a solar power station, giant mirrors (above) concentrate the Sun's heat and use it to boil water, to make electricity.

hydroelectric power   electricity made using the energy from moving water

Hydroelectric power

Moving water has a lot of energy. At a hydroelectric power station, a **dam** is built across a river to make a lake. The water is allowed to flow through the dam, turning turbines that then turn the **generators**.

▼ About 25 percent of the world's electricity is made using hydroelectric power.

Solar cells

Solar cells change sunlight energy into electricity. These houses in the Netherlands (above) are powered by the solar cells on their roofs.

dam   barrier built across a river to make a lake to store water

Benefits of using fossil fuels:

- **Fossil fuels** have a lot of **energy** in them. This is easily released as heat and light energy by burning.

- **Power stations** that use fossil fuels are easily and quickly started.

- Coal is easy to move using trucks, trains, or ships.

- Oil and natural gas can be moved along pipelines and stored easily in tanks.

Keep searching

As supplies of fossil fuels become more scarce, we will have to search further for them. New oil fields are usually in faraway places (above). The new roads, pipelines, and refineries that are built to use them often damage the environment in wild and beautiful places.

► When oil tankers have accidents at sea, birds and other animals get covered in thick, sticky oil.

Problems of using fossil fuels:

- Fuels made from oil are dangerous to transport because they can catch fire easily.

- Fossil fuels are **nonrenewable** so they will run out one day.

- Fossil fuels cause **pollution** when they burn, which causes **global warming**.

- Oil spills cause lots of damage to the **environment**.

In the future, our electricity will be **generated** in many different ways. Until then, scientists will keep looking for new places to find fossil fuels and at other types of **renewable** energy.

◄ This electric car makes electricity using hydrogen fuel.

Find Out More

Further Reading

Hunter, Rebecca. *Energy (Discovering Science)*. Chicago: Raintree, 2001.

Miller, Kimberly M. *What If We Run Out of Fossil Fuels?* New York: Children's Press, 2002.

Oxlade, Chris. *Energy (Science Topics)*. Chicago: Heinemann Library, 1999

Sneddon, Robert. *Energy From Fossil Fuels (Essential Energy)*. Chicago: Heinemann Library, 2001.

World Wide Web

To find out more about **fossil fuels,** you can search the Internet. Use keywords like these:

- "fossil fuels"
- coal +mining
- oil +refining
- oil +uses
- "tar pit"
- "natural gas"

You can find your own keywords by using words from this book. The search tips opposite will help you find the most useful web sites.

Organizations

Fossil Fuels
Environmental Literacy Council
An organization dedicated to helping young people make informed choices about their impact on the environment. This site has links providing an introduction to fossil fuels, their use, available supplies, and prospects for the future.

Contact them at:
1625 K Street, NW, Suite 1020
Washington, DC 20006-3868

Search tips

There are billions of pages on the Internet. It can be difficult to find exactly what you are looking for. These tips will help you find useful web sites more quickly:

- Use simple keywords.
- Use two to six keywords in a search.
- Only use names of people, places, or things.
- Put double quote marks around words that go together, for example, "solar power"

Where to search

Search engine

A search engine looks through millions of web site pages. It lists all the sites that match the words in the search box. You will find that the best matches are at the top of the list, on the first page.

Search directory

A person instead of a computer has sorted a search directory. You can search by keyword or subject and browse through the different sites. It is like looking through books on a library shelf.

Glossary

acid rain rain that contains substances that damage buildings and living things

atmosphere layer of gases surrounding Earth

atom tiny bit from which everything is made

bog waterlogged and spongy wetland

carbon type of chemical

coalface part of a coal seam that is being cut away

condense change from a gas to a liquid

conveyor belt rubber strip that moves objects along

dam barrier built across a river to make a lake to store water

dissolve when a solid or a gas mixes with water

energy being able to do work. Light, heat, and electricity are types of energy

energy resource something from which we can get useful amounts of energy

environment the world around us

evaporate change from a liquid into a gas

filter device that allows some substances to pass through it, but not others

fossil fuel fuel formed from the remains of ancient plants and animals

fossilized turned into stone

fraction one of the different substances in oil

generate make or produce

generator machine that makes electricity

geothermal anything to do with heat from deep underground

global warming extra warming of Earth caused by an increased greenhouse effect

greenhouse effect how Earth's atmosphere keeps the planet warm

hydroelectric power electricity made using the energy from moving water

Industrial Revolution period of rapid development in industry in the late 1700s and early 1800s

landfill waste site

mineral substance needed by plants and animals to keep them healthy

molecule tiny particle of a substance

molten melted

neutralize make a substance neutral, not acid or alkali

nonporous does not let liquids and gases through

nonrenewable will run out one day and can never be replaced

nuclear using energy from atoms

oilfield reservoir of oil underground

particle tiny piece of something

pesticide chemical that kills insects and other pests that harm crops

pollute make air, water, or land dirty and dangerous